Inte

PRAYERS AND REFLECTIONS OF A SERVANT

Interludes...
PRAYERS AND REFLECTIONS OF A SERVANT'S HEART

MICHAEL J. EASLEY

MOODY PUBLISHERS
CHICAGO

© 2005 by MICHAEL J. EASLEY

All rights reserved. No part of this book may be reproduced in any form without permission in writing from the publisher, except in the case of brief quotations embodied in critical articles or reviews.

All Scripture quotations, unless otherwise indicated, are taken from the *New American Standard Bible*®. Copyright © The Lockman Foundation 1960, 1962, 1963, 1968, 1971, 1972, 1973, 1975, 1977, 1995. Used by permission.

Scripture quotations marked ESV are taken from *The Holy Bible, English Standard Version*. Copyright © 2000, 2001 by Crossway Bibles, a division of Good News Publishers. Used by permission. All rights reserved.

ISBN: 0-8024-4708-2
ISBN-13: 978-0-8024-4708-1

1 3 5 7 9 10 8 6 4 2

Printed in the United States of America

For Cindy
"an excellent wife"

The Lonely Place

BUT JESUS OFTEN WITHDREW TO LONELY PLACES AND PRAYED.
—LUKE 5:16

Perhaps nothing is more difficult than prayer.

For followers of Jesus, we describe efforts to pray with phrases like

> *I wrestle with prayer*
> *I struggle to pray*
> *My prayer life is weak*
> *All my prayers sound the same*
> *I know I should pray more*
> *I don't pray enough*
> *I don't know how to pray*
> *I fall asleep when I pray*
> *Praying is boring*
> *I tried but I just can't pray*
> *I used to pray, but it did not work*

❧

Dr. Howard G. Hendricks, distinguished professor for over fifty years, editorialized, "Hold a conference on

prophecy and people come out by droves. Hold a conference on prayer and people stay away by the thousands."

On another occasion, Dr. Hendricks queried, "Did it
ever occur to you that there is only one thing the gospels
record, when the disciples asked Jesus to teach them something? They asked Jesus to *teach* them to pray. What does
this reveal of the disciples' struggle?"

Over the years, many have tried to help us, teach us,
and encourage us to pray. Devotionals, daily readings,
prayer books, journals, entries from saints of other genera-
tions, mystical intrigue, and studies have been produced to
cheer us on to pray. Call it a discipline, devotion, duty, or
even religion—it seems that only silver-haired widows know
the richness and joy of prayer.

My journey with prayer may be like yours. On rare
occasions, I think I am praying well. Most of the time, I
know I do not have a clue about prayer. I can quickly feel
guilty about not praying. I can muster up a good habit for
a while, but praying for lists of sick people does not keep
me motivated. This may say more about my personal
issues, but I find many believers pale to prayer. So, perhaps
like you, I have read books on prayer, kept prayer lists,
studied prayer in the Bible, and kept prayer journals. (The
quirkiest attempt was to record prayer requests and
answers in an unused checkbook register, dating the
request and answer like a deposit and withdrawal.)

So maybe we visit a prayer meeting or a prayer service.
As a pastor, it is a horrible admission to make, but I
hate prayer meetings. Think about the last prayer meeting
you attended:

· We spend more time talking about requests than praying
· We share concerns (code language for "gossip" and "worry")
· We pray about generic items: travel safety, health, upcoming surgeries, jobs
· We pray through a list of unknown people (the hallowed "unspoken requests")
· If we pray about other things, it is about someone else's prodigal son, a friend of a friend's marriage, a distant relative's problems
· Maybe we pray for things like church leaders, unity, people coming to Christ, and missions
· And we lament with the prophets of old, and pray that other people would be more committed and come to our prayer meeting

All of these are fine concerns. I do not mean to demean. We are instructed to pray for all things. And very committed believers faithfully come to prayer meetings and are serious and devout in their prayers. Yet if this is supposed to be vital, crucial, essential, the warp and woof of a believer's soul, why does it still fall flat for the great majority of believers?

Prayer can feel like a wedding reception of people you do not know very well but among whom you have to be on your best behavior. It seems more like a tedious gathering than Gethsemane, more like coffee and fellowship than Paul's prayer for enlightenment.

I hold several convictions about prayer. You may not agree with all of these, and if not, I hope you will develop your own. But these are mine:

- A personal prayer life is more important than group or public prayer
- The discipline or development of prayer is an indicator of growth, maturity, and intimacy with Christ
- Prayer is a relationship, not a task
- Prayer is recognition that my dependence is not partial but total
- Our prayer "life" will wax and wane
- Pain, suffering, and problems may well be God's motivators for us to pray
- Eloquence in prayer is not important
- Prayer is communication with the Creator of the universe. As a result, why use repetitious, dull, canned language to talk with God?
- Choosing good words, expressions, phrases that clearly articulate prayer is important
- Keeping a journal or writing prayers helps us see, over time, more about ourselves than whether God "answers" prayer
- If prayer is important to Christ, would He leave His followers in a fog for all time?

As the Mennonites urged, *pray until you have prayed.*

—MICHAEL J. EASLEY

~ *Again* ~

Lord Who sustains

Again I come to You for grace
      Grace that kept me overnight
      Grace that keeps me this moment
      Grace that will keep me tomorrow

Again I move "in but not of"
      where my affections will be tempted
      My head will be turned
      My heart will be deceived
      My motives twisted
      My will overused

Again, I need You, every moment, every step, every glance
      I offer nothing good apart from You
      I only harm others and myself
      I always rebel

Again, I need
      Your Spirit's control
      Your power to resist
      Your Word to guide

~ *Everyday* ~

Great Provider and only Creator,

Help us every day to know that You
    Gave to us in our sleep
    Renewed our weary frames in the night
    Presented us with a new start—every morning

Help us every day to remember You
    Provide a roof
    Supply us with nourishment
    Protect us with clothing
    All of which—to our shame—we take for granted

Remind us when we forget that You
    Heal us when we are sick
    Nourish us when we (greedily) consume
    Supply us when we freely spend
    Use us—even though we sin—for Your glory

Forgive us every day when we
    Hurry into busyness
    Disregard appointments with You
    Rush past You with self-importance
    Think our lives are more important than You

Help us have a constant awareness
    That Jesus has covered all our sins
    That as unlovely as we may feel, Jesus loves us
    That forgiveness cost immeasurably
    That our lives can be more about Jesus and less
    about us
    That our lives can be an ongoing "Thank You" for
    Your grace, righteousness, mercy, and love.

~ Those Who Followed ~

Your disciples followed
They saw Your power
They witnessed You
Yet they were afraid

They saw You
Face to face
Sweat to sweat
Land to water
Death to life
Yet doubted

They heard You
Touched You
Knew You
Were Your friends
Yet vacillated

May we follow well
Not turning to the side
Walking the path straight
Keeping the narrow way
With an eye to the light

Hold my hand to Your plow
Keep my back to the sun
My face like flint
Directing my heart to serve You, and You alone.

So when I am weighed in the balance
I will have been a good and faithful follower
Of my Lord, my Jesus, my Christ.

~ *You/We* ~

Eternal Father, Three-in-One:

You have existed from and in all eternity
We exist only in Your choice (before the foundation
of the world)

You have created and sustain Your creation
We can only live within Your creation

You have always been the Father to the Son
We are only sons because You are the adopting Father

You have designed space, time, life, and death
We only inch near knowledge

You have been enthroned for all time
We watch one generation erase another

You order unbendable laws of this realm
We play with and pretend we understand Your ways

You have not changed
We bend with winds of fashion

You are always with us
We are great risks of flight

You love the unlovely
We, the unlovely, seldom love

Your holiness and glory set You apart
We smudge and smear all that is good

You give, bless, forgive, and hear
We take, demand, blame, and forget

Your Son has made the way
We require Your Spirit to compass our hearts

Your Son has obeyed in every and all ways
We need Your Spirit to obey at all

Holy Father, Three-in-One, according to the kind intention of Your will, help us be Your faithful children, heirs to an indescribable eternity with You. For apart from You, we can do nothing.

We Honor God when we

ask for great things.

It is a humiliating thing

to think we are satisfied

with very small results.

—D. L. Moody

The "I Love Me" Wall

He is pretty matter-of-fact about it all, but his was a prestigious career as a naval pilot. He ended his tour with a successful command, and rather than move yet again—flag in sight—he got out of the Navy and gave the moving vans (and his wife) a rest. It has been several years now, and he does not talk about it much. Once I visited his home and on a basement wall hung records of achievement—all kinds of awards, plaques, medals, and citations. Apparently at one time these trophies were pretty important to him because they had been nicely matted and framed. I asked about them and he said with a deflecting smile, "Everyone has an 'I love me wall.'" One time he did tell me what kind of jet was in a particular picture, but that was all. He still won't tell you anything about them.

I got to wondering about this "I love me wall." Some display sheepskins. Some have sports trophies. Some have a rack from a buck, or a large bass. For some, it might be their kids, their prom photo, or their wedding day. Lots of things can be a display of "I love me."

John 15 is weighted with many profound issues. The vine imagery has theologians still scratching their heads. Significant concepts in the chapter include *prune* and clean, *abide* (occurring about ten times), *keep My commandments*, *love* (eight times) and others. It is a body of crucial concepts the Master gave us.

One that struck me was Jesus' notice to His disciples—His close friends—that "apart from Me you can do nothing" (v. 5). At least we can understand that the vine imagery and abiding mean there is a relationship between the disciples' doing what Jesus wants them to do and their total inability to do it apart from Him. He's telling them to abide, and there is some sense in which they choose to abide—yet He is the vine. He wants them to "bear much fruit" (v. 8), and that somehow that proves them to be His followers. Then in verses 9–13 "love" becomes the operative term. If they "keep His commandments" they abide in His love. Then He gives them the commandment in verse 12, that they "love one another, just as I have loved you."

~ Because ~

I love the Lord because[1]
> He listens to my prayers
> He hears my complaints
> He knows my longings
> He does not reject me when I am stupid

Help me, great auditor
> To admit and confess my transgression
> To embrace and own my sin
> To examine and uncover my defensiveness
> To lay the blame at my feet, not others'

Empower me, great Sovereign
> To keep close to You in my "dailyness"
> To call on You when trouble begins
> To rest in You and not my machinations
> To confess, admit, and acknowledge my guilt

Remind me, patient Father
> That my salvation is secure
> That while men fail, You do not
> That I serve You, not myself
> And that I can only offer thanks because of you.

[1] *Cp. Psalm 116:1–2*

~ The Problem with Self ~

It calls for attention
Craves it
Demands it
Longs for it
Becomes jealous when ignored

How can it not be
Always, always about Me?

I am to do nothing from selfishness
I am not to be conceited
I am to be humble
I am to regard others more important than Me.[2]

[2] *Cp. Philippians 2:3–8*

~ The Distracted Traveler ~

Father, Maker of time

Move my mind from the droning routines of my life,
To an increasing occupation of captive thoughts toward You.

Forgive my *here and now* focus that excludes
You from my heart,
Forgive my frantic activities that crowd
You from my mind,
Forgive my penchant to busy myself with
distractions far greater than Martha's,
Forgive my sin-sick self and its unyielding
demand for attention.

You have created every day.
You have allotted to me a number of days.
You have ordered all my days.
You have created every day I take for granted.
You have permitted every day for which I demand more.
You have given me great freedom in the use of these
fleeting minutes, hours, days, and weeks.
You have known before the foundation of the world,
what lies in wait for me.
You have measured out grace in time in every step of my life.

Please, by Your powerful Holy Spirit,
Help this distracted traveler.
Help me to calm when details demand attention.
Help me to rest when I see mountains of tasks that
will never be done.

Help me to once in a while think a little less of me
and a little more of You.
Help me not to live this life in the horizontal, never
slowing or resting long enough to see Your vertical vistas.

Ever patient Father, maker of time, what will it take
for me to live as You want me to live,
Rather than my penchant for clamor and anxiety?
It will require nothing less than Your very presence.
It will require Your grace—yet again—to this distracted saint.
It will require You to measure out mercy like a paycheck—
to give to me what I need more than want.
Yet, since you indulge your distracted saint this far, will
I ever be released from my horizontal fixation?

O God of time, release me from this dailyness and grant me
once in a while, times where You transcend me from my
routines that cleverly chain me to the mundane.
For what if I live this life so unfocused on the next?
What if I live this life so fixated on distractions?
What if I live this life anxious, busy, frenetic?
How will I face eternity with You?

Would you in mercy measure more to help me?

Inching Toward Peace

Over the years, I have struggled with anxiety a lot. In God's great kindness, I see it less and less in my soul, but at times it creeps in like kudzu. I've been dealing with my own "stuff" with an anxiety that is less the panicky kind and more of a sense of feeling torn and pulled. So today, I returned to the shopworn Philippians 4:6–7 for relief and found none. Not because the text is inadequate—but because I am in rebellion. But, that said, I found myself inching toward "peace" and "rest" in the oft-overlooked context, verses 8–9. Interesting instruction to "dwell on these things" that refer to what I'd call the "whatever . . ." list. Take a look at it—and ponder a bit. May His Word refresh us all and help us confidently rest IN HIM, not our machinations. I kind of "diagramed" the verse a little:

≫

Philippians 4:6–9
Be anxious for nothing, but in everything by prayer and supplication with thanksgiving let your requests be made known to God. And the peace of God, which surpasses all comprehension, will guard your hearts and your minds in Christ Jesus.

Finally, brethren,

> whatever is true,

> whatever is honorable,

> whatever is right,

> whatever is pure,

> whatever is lovely,

> whatever is of good repute,

> if there is any excellence and if anything worthy of praise, dwell on these things.

The things you have learned and received and heard and seen in me, practice these things, and the God of peace will be with you.

- Living Dead -

Why do I live like dead men

In Christ I have been
   Made alive
   Granted eternal life
   Promised eternity

~ Idols for Destruction ~

Sovereign God and Father, who displaces all idols
Displace the idols of my heart.
Remove my constructs from the mantel of my mind.
Dash to pieces the metals I would polish and adore.
If drinking their dust would cure me from adoration,
I would gladly ingest them.

Why, O soul, do you turn your attention toward
all that glitters?
Why, O soul, do you coddle that which gives no warmth?
Why, O soul, do you embrace a title, position, or
rank that cannot love back?
Why, O soul, do you worship lifeless trophies that
can offer no life in return?
Why, O soul, do you trade yesterday's idol for
tomorrow's new ones?

One and Only Savior, be pronounced to my affections.
One and Only Lord, dismantle the shelves that hold
trophies of dust.
One and Only Christ, lift up my head to worship, serve,
adore, and place all my affections on You and You alone.

By Your powerful Holy Spirit, give me the arsenal
to defend.
By Your powerful Holy Spirit, equip me to not only
say "no," but to say "yes" to You.
By Your powerful Holy Spirit, grant me a tenacity,
a discipline and, if I do not beg too much, a joy in
serving You that overwhelms any affections toward
lifeless toys.

O God and Father, the only true God, help me to
love You and You alone.
Help me, lest I build another shelf. . . .

~ A Theologue's Prayer ~

Loved.
Chosen.
Rescued.
Forgiven.

Redeemed.
Justified.
Adopted.
Sealed.

Declared.
Indwelt.
Empowered.
Imputed.

Pursued.
Reconciled.
Reckoned.
Sanctified.

Tested.
Refined.
Encouraged.
Strengthened.

Convicted.
Disciplined.
Chastened.
Rebuked.

Transformed.
Blessed.
Seated.
Graced.

Pardoned.
Purified.
Released.
Liberated.

Renewed.
Consecrated.
Commissioned.
Loved.

I DO NOT KNOW

WHAT PRAYER IS;

I ONLY KNOW

THAT PRAYER IS.

—GHERT BAHANNA

What Is Prayer?

A lot of factors contribute to our understanding of prayer. If we were raised in a religious tradition, we tend to have perspectives on prayer that may or may not be helpful. If we had no religious exposure, then we may have assembled different ideas about what prayer is or is not.

Prayer is at once
- Worship
- Commanded (Ephesians 6:18; 1 Thessalonians 5:17)
- Communication (speaking and listening)
- Devotion (Acts 2:42; 6:4; Colossians 4:2)
- Discipline (Matthew 6:6; 14:23; Mark 1:35)
- Thankfulness (Romans 1:8–12; Philippians 4:6)
- Intercession (1 Thessalonians 1:2ff; Ephesians 1:16ff)
- Relationship (Luke 5:16; 6:12; Hebrews 4:14–16; 5:7–8; 10:22)
- Dependence (1 Samuel 1:15)
- Asking (Matthew 7:7; John 14:13–14; Acts 12:5; 1 Timothy 2:1)
- Taught and learned (Luke 11:1)
- Others?

~ A Parent's Plea ~

Perfect Father of all mankind, help.

Perfect Father of the first and second Adam, help me to parent these unique souls placed into my care.

> May I not exasperate them.
> May I not ignore them.
> May I not withdraw from them.
> May I not be worn down by them.
> May I not retreat from the battle for their hearts.
> May I not bear on them too hard or too long.
> May I not ridicule or mock their forming hearts.
> May I not dismiss or break their hopes.

Unique Father, Perfect Parent, help me to submit to You and grow up as Your child.

> May I listen to them with discerning wisdom.
> May I see beyond their "presenting problem" and peer into their hearts and souls.
> May I have a firmness and gentleness that never makes them fearful but always makes them safe.
> May I have the patience of Job and the endurance of Paul no matter how long the journey.
> May I love them until they know it.
> May I help them until they can do it on their own.
> May I equip them to handle Your Word.

May I encourage, build up, and nurture their faith
to be more secure than mine.
May I have the humility to believe more for them
than I did for me.
May I tell them and tell them and tell them of Your
love for them.
May I place my comforts, wants, desires, dreams,
and longings aside to show them the kind of love
You have for us.
May I be terrified and cautious knowing that I shape
their view of You from the moment they came into
my home to the moment they leave it.

O God, Perfect Father, Only God, help, for I am a desper-
ately incapable man. Resolve my fear, my longing, my
inadequacy, my flight and enable me to be Your man
to parent these precious souls.

~ A Preacher's Petition ~

Great God of the Word
Who spoke creation into existence
Who spoke covenants to men
Who spoke laws of life
Speak through
  the thick of tongue
  the slow of mind
  the dull of heart
  the justified yet sinful soul

May I always know these are Your people
May I always see sheep without a shepherd
May I always see the blend of
  lost travelers
  broken hearts
  young in faith
  and faithful servants

How can a man speak for God?
Even angels know better than to open their mouth with
less than verbatim.
How can a man—for a lifetime—help others know You?
Even prophets were ignored and dismissed.
How can a man explain the eternal?
Even the apostle was thought a fool.

May I always be found in Your text.
May I always be grounded in Your precepts.
May I always be moored to Your Word.
May I always be accused of teaching Scripture.

Keep my head and heart toward You.
Keep me in the world but not of it.
Help me never to bore Your people with Your Word.
Help me never breath stale air from living language
Help me never pour brackish water
when cool rushing streams are nearby.

If my life models anything, let it be a longing to be close
to You.

And when my tour is over
The last sermon endured
The last words said
May they remember You and Your Word
And may they always demand, "Sir, we would see Jesus!"

~ Protect Us ~

(Prayer given before the U.S. House of Representatives)

Creator, Sovereign, Lord of all, help us.
Even though we do not deserve it,
We ask for Your mercy
We ask humbly that You would please bless the country
that we so dearly love.

Protect us from our enemies
    We ask not merely for ourselves, but for our children
    We ask not merely for our children,
    but for their children

Protect us from ourselves
    May we never
        exercise the strength of tyrants
        misuse talents entrusted to us
        or lord over those allotted to our charge

We pray for our president, his family, his cabinet
    We thank You for him.
    Give him otherworldly wisdom
    Give him enduring strength
    Give him friends who speak truth
    Give him rest
    And draw him ever closer to You

We pray for our men and women overseas,
keeping an oath they swore
    Their families who keep watch and prayer
    Our civil servants who protect and rescue us
    All who lead, govern, and serve our country
    Our marriages, families, purity, common sense and
    a moral restraint in keeping with Your covenants.

Dear God of faithful promise and gifts
    Thank You that You love the unlovely
    Thank You that You look at us and see Your Son.
    And thank You that You even hear our prayers.

In Jesus' name, Amen.

PEPOLE WHO PRAY

LONG IN PUBLIC

PRAY LITTLE

IN PRIVATE.

—CHARLES SPURGEON

How to Be Like Clarence Thomas

I once read an article in the *Washingtonian* magazine about how rarely Supreme Court Justice Clarence Thomas speaks. The piece also critiqued those who talk a lot. As one of the latter, it made me wince. But I really wince when I read one of the many Proverbs that addresses the mouth—and when to keep it shut: "He who despises his neighbor lacks sense [literally, "heart"], but a man of understanding keeps silent" (Proverbs 11:12).

This came to mind a while back when I was still in the pastorate and often involved in some challenging and complex meetings. Some were meetings with staff; some involved my having to evaluate others. Overall, these meetings were healthy, helpful, and good, but they did require addressing some . . . issues.

One thing that amazes me is how we let things go too long before addressing them—and this is where the "talking problem" comes in. Rather than address the person directly and deal with the immediate concern, we go off-line and chat with others about our "neighbor." It is so easy to talk *about* someone—it is so difficult to talk *with* her or him. Seems to me this Proverb is assailing me when I speak ill of my neighbor—when rather, if I was a "man of understanding," I would keep silent.

Whether you are in a work setting, a church setting, a school setting, dealing with extended family, or facing some other interpersonal difficulty . . . here are some ideas for you. And for me. I can . . .

- Ask the Holy Spirit to help me bite my lip.
- Know when to keep my mouth shut.
- Walk away from the coffeepot conversation.
- Leave the copy room when the whispers begin. (I wonder if whispering equals some conversation that should not be taking place?)
- Avoid conversations "about" someone.
- And, if you are like me (God help you), try to be a little more like Justice Thomas.

~ We Are Only ~

High and holy Father
Who condescended to man
Meek and lowly Savior
Who exalted to You
We come only because You granted access

We are only called because You call
We are only blessed because You bless
We are only chosen because You chose
And we are only redeemed because You redeem

Keep us from the duplicity of legalism
Guard us from the pretense of pride
Shape us into useful clay
Employ us in the kingdom's call

Free us from fears that immobilize
Empower us by Your Spirit's grace
And confirm in us the work of Your hand

May we be found
Hands to the plow
Hearts toward Your Throne
And smiling as we serve

We ask in the Name above all Names
Christ, Your only Son.

~ Silence ~

When [He] broke the seventh seal,
there was silence in heaven for about half an hour.
Revelation 8:1

Who are You, this Jesus?
Who are You, this Lamb?
Who are You, this Worthy One?
You are The One.

Silence.

Hustle, hurry, deadlines await.
Pressure, stress, self-important me.
Tasks, briefs, helping others.
Burdens, problems, sweating for bread.

Silence.

Traffic, schedules, jobs to do.
Crisis, whining, selfish others.
Broken stuff, repairs clamor, too much to do.
Overweight, out of shape, heavy loads.

Silence.

When will you be quiet?
When will you listen?
When will you stop?
When will you be silent?

One day, the heavens will be quiet.
Still.
Undisturbed.
Pensive.
And then, all hell will start to break loose.

I wonder, why do we say so much
When we have nothing to say?

Enthroned Lamb
The One true Shepherd
Help me to be silent once in a while.

DEVOTE YOURSELF TO PRAYER,

KEEPING ALERT IN IT

WITH AN ATTITUDE

OF THANKSGIVING.

—1 THESSALONIANS 1:2

A Few Books That Help Me Pray

The "Christian solution" for everything in life seems to be a book. We talk with a friend about a problem or question or an idea and he says, "Have you read _____?" We share books, buy books, stack them up on end tables—and a few might get read. So, there are zero guarantees any "book" is going to help anyone pray.

The books that are noted here may or may not be of help to you. If I have learned anything about prayer, it is that certain things help at certain times but nothing helps all the time. At first, this is frustrating. Understood differently, it can be incredibly freeing. What books do offer are ideas, thoughts, suggestions, and perspectives that neither you nor I would probably discover if left alone for a hundred years. If a book gives you several new ideas, clarifying thoughts, or a more precise perspective, then it has been a good investment of the mind.

Andrew Murray, *Christ in the School of Prayer*
E.M. Bounds, *Power and Purpose in Prayer*
Richard Strauss, *Sense and Nonsense about Prayer*

The Valley of Vision, a collection of Puritan prayers and devotions, edited by Arthur Bennett (The Banner of Truth

Trust, 1975), has proven to be a watershed in my prayer life. Seldom have I read one or two prayers at most and not found myself lost in the wonder and depth of these saints' love for God and recognition of their deep disappointment with their own sins. Somewhere in between the extremes of self-hatred and self-love, these men and women sought a spiritual place unknown in our time. Recognizing our deepest depravity and yet calling on the grace of God seem to be bookmarks of these prayers.

Unlike other devotions, *The Valley of Vision* usually penetrates the head *and* heart. My copy has become worn with marks, tears, puzzlement, and promise. I find it a warm and friendly companion to the Word of God most every day.

~ Praise God Because of His Works ~
(Psalm 111)

Make a choice to praise Him.
Tell your heart to give thanks.
Tell others to do the same.

The Lord, Maker, Creator, and Sustainer
Has displayed majesty in His works.
The casual man will ignore them.
The curious man will consider them.
The wise man will study them.
The worshiper can delight in them.

The Lord, Maker, Creator, and Sustainer
Has shown Himself in marvelous ways.
    Lights of the sky reveal His brilliance
    Creatures of the air, water, and land exhibit
    His life giving
    Plants bear fruit of His provision
    But man reflects His image

Those who know Him will see
Those who love Him will give thanks
Those who know their condition will worship Him.

He has told us.
He has shown us.
He has remembered us.

He has provided for us.
Do we yet doubt?
Do we still disbelieve?
Much worse, do we forget?

Daily He gives to us
    Food in portion
    Sleep in measure
    Health in doses
    Breath without number

Does He not faithfully show us?
Does He not consistently sustain us?
Does He not daily give bread?

Why then do we doubt the greater things?
    Is He not gracious and compassionate?
    Is He not loving and kind?
    Is He not holy and just?
    Does He not remember?

His Word is sure and true.
His Word is immovable.
His Word is redemption.
His Word is as good as His name.
His Word revealed Him and established His works.

Make a choice to praise Him.
Tell your heart to give thanks.
Tell others to do the same.

Manifold!

Some friends of mine visited Austria years ago. Upon their return, they gave me a small crystal paperweight. The clarity of this crystal was astonishing. It was essentially perfect in every way. Held one way, you could look straight through it and the image on the other side was undistorted. Yet if you turned it slightly, the prismatic plays of light delighted your eyes. The word "manifold" comes to mind. "Manifold" can mean many, varied, in so many ways, unspeakably rich. To hold this crystal at arms' length and turn it displayed manifold beauty.

Scripture is rich in theology, narrative, language, emotion, meaning, and covers an eternal perspective on mankind's condition and God's righteousness. The Bible is *manifold* in giving us clarity about God and our relationship to Him.

When we read and study the Bible, the careful student discovers this manifold gem. Since the Word is lavish and marvelous, we confidently conclude the Father of the universe is intelligent, wise, and brilliant beyond human description. If true, why would we pray with meaningless repetition, cliché phrases, worn-out words? It is not as though God will hear better if we pray better. But if we are bland and boring in our prayer, it certainly reflects our perspective of our God and may be diagnostic as to why we are poor at prayer.

An accurate view of our Father will alter our prayers.

~ *Compassionate Counselor* ~

Why are you in despair, O my soul?
And why are you disturbed within me?
Hope in God, for I shall again praise Him,
The help of my countenance and my God.
Psalm 43:5

When I am sullen or withdrawn
My face is a pretense of empathy and interest
And I am far away from You, Your people, Your Spirit,
and Your grace

When I am stern, unsympathetic, or indifferent
My secret feelings are critical and impatient of others
These judgmental attitudes discolor my perception
and energy

Not only do You care for all Your people
You care for me in my careless condition

Thank You that You
    Do not let me get away with sinful thoughts
    Reveal my repulsive feelings toward those
    You died for
    Are merciful and patient with the lost and the found
    Love me enough to convict and discipline me

While I will never be You, make me as You
    Compassionate and caring
    Loving and enduring
    Firm and tender

How can You forgive this one who is so stiff-necked?
How can You love this one who is so unlovely?
How can You endure one so impatient?
How can You consider one so petty?
How can You have compassion on one so compassionless?

Your Son bore the wrath that I deserved
You loved immeasurably
Help me never understand and always be broken
And yet, I beg, give me Your joy

For when I consider You, why would I ever not hope?

~ O Faithful Lord ~

Who Adam should have trusted
Who Abraham should have trusted
Who Isaac should have trusted
Who Jacob should have trusted
Who Moses should have trusted
Who David should have trusted

O faithful Lord, who is trustworthy
Why did our fathers trust but not trust?
Why do we not trust and rest in You?

Forgive me for judging others' failures
Forgive me for answering like a Pharisee
Forgive me for considering others weak

You are great and faithful
You are holy and righteous
You are the hope of all who seek You

Yet we languish at the first sweat of faith
We whine at the first delay
We withdraw at the first obstacle
We tire at the first hour
We wander at the first lonely watch
We cry at first pain

O great and faithful Lord
What will it take to believe You
What will it take to rest in You
What will it take to trust when we cannot see You
What will it take to know You are God and we are not?

By faith, help us to choose to
Endure when we weary
Resist when tempted
Mature when complacent
Serve when selfish
Be joyful when depressed

O great and faithful Lord
Grant to us, not just a miracle,
but an immovable faith.

~ For the Fidgety Soul ~

I waited patiently for the LORD;
And he inclined to me and heard my cry.
Psalm 40:1

Dear God in heaven, how infrequent is my waiting patiently.
Even in mild dismay, I do not wait.
>   My hands wring.
>   My feet hurry.
>   My mind races.
>   My heart angers.
>   My self wants to do, fix, resolve.

I do not want to wait, nor do I want to wait in You.
>   How did David so patiently wait?
>   How can You so patiently wait?

I dare not ask for patient waiting, lest You leave me in a pit.
>   I pull back my hand as from a knife.
>   I turn my soul from the life giver.
>   I hedge my heart from quiet voids.
>   I show myself a childish fool.

Though I despise the in-between, it is the place
You leave me.
    Help me know when it is not discipline.
    Teach me that rest is good for the unknown
    road ahead.
    Quiet my anxious, foolish, self-sufficient delusions.

And when You pause my life, I sheepishly ask
    Stretch out Your grace to this fidgety soul
    Bend Your mercy toward a wriggling heart
    Incline Your ear my way
    Listen to the voice of Your impatient child

And may I truly know, like David,
That You have heard my cry.

AFTER HE HAD SENT

THE CROWDS AWAY,

HE WENT UP ON THE MOUNTAIN

BY HIMSELF TO PRAY;

AND WHEN IT WAS EVENING,

HE WAS THERE ALONE.

—MATTHEW 26:39—41

What's It Worth to You?

BETTER IS A POOR MAN WHO WALKS IN HIS INTEGRITY THAN
HE WHO IS PERVERSE IN SPEECH AND IS A FOOL.
— PROVERBS 19:1

I am motivated by money.

OK, I said it. Not that I dream of wealth. Not that I wish I were rich. Not that I am real jealous of others who have "stuff" I don't have. I just wonder sometimes what it would be like to have all the stuff I want. If I wanted to make lots of money, I would have picked a different profession. And there are always those who make a lot more—and a lot less—than I do.

Too often, I think a thing will make me happier. I can even cloak it in language of "being thankful to God that He has 'blessed' me." Or, "Thanks, Lord, for the provision of the (thing I want) that will make my (ministry, hobby, life) so much better." That is sick. Sure, God gives to us lavishly, and we must acknowledge that everything we have is from His hand. (Even though we might have some stuff that He'd rather we not have.) But ultimately, is not the job, money, acquisition possible because of His allowance?

This whole notion is woven into the fabric of the

so-called American dream. It is so much part of the warp and woof of our culture, education, society, and lineage that I doubt many Americans can ever unravel it out of their soul. We hated the prosperity theology of televangelism; but secretly, I think a lot of believers hold to the notion that "if I live right, God will 'bless' me." And we just might be thinking about money, promotions, and . . . stuff.

This dangling proverb tells us a lot. For one, it tells me it is better to be poor than perverse (crooked, deceptive, twisted) in my words. It is better to be poor than a fool. But here it links "poor" with one who walks in his integrity.

Maybe the point of this rambling is: Integrity is the greatest wealth you can possess. Want to be wealthy? Pursue integrity. Want to have "riches"? Be a man/woman of integrity. The Hebrew stem suggests "blameless"—something you can't put a finger on. The Latin apparently borrowed the term and made *integer* out of it: a whole number. What encourages me is that *this* wealth is attainable to every believer! Any one of us can walk in integrity. Any one of us can live clean. Any one of us can choose this wealth.

I have always been struck by David's choice, his deliberate commitment in Psalm 101:2-3: "I will walk within my house in the integrity of my heart. I will set no worthless thing before my eyes." And I wonder, what "worthless thing" do I set in front of my eyes? What TV show have I watched that was "worth-while"? What magazine? What book? What shopping mall? What bill-board? What computer screen image?

Place inestimable value on integrity. Integrity is the greatest wealth you can possess. It is available to everyone, even the "poor." And last time I checked, there were a lot more poor people in the world than "rich."

~ How Can I Be ~

Ezekiel 18:30–32

How can I be pure in heart?

I cannot see, feel, know, or be confident of any good thing in me. My eyes, senses, and mind pull me to sin like insatiable hunger.

How I long to be Your man, Your disciple, Your own, yet in a thousand ways with a thousand excuses, I tempt fate, walk too close to sin, fall off the precarious edge into sin's offers.

A lie. It is all a lie. Each sin that pulls at my eyes, loins or mind promises something it can never deliver. Yet I am self deceived, self deluded, self degraded.

How can I be pure in heart?

O gracious otherworldly Father, forgive—yet again—the willful choice to sin.

My sins are not indiscretions; they are violent offenses to You.

My sins are not infractions in need of censure, but crimes deserving punishment.

My sins are not ever taken lightly by You . . . why do I take them lightly when entertaining them in my heart? Would I take lightly the injustice and punishment of Your innocent Son? Would I raise my hand in hatred and self-justification and strike at Him? Yes, a thousand times, yes. For in each and any way I toy with sin, I confess my hatred and contempt for Your perfect Son, Jesus.

How can I be pure in heart?

When my impatience rages with people with whom I do not care or give myself to their concerns.

When my self-centeredness breaks my concentration from someone else to my own needs.

When my fear and insecurity tempts me to think I could ever be "smart" or "sufficient."

When my lusts play with thoughts too shameful to think, much less write.

When my ego and pride lie to me yet again that I am "important" or "unimportant"—both of which dismiss the work of new creation.

How can I be pure in heart?

Your Spirit is available, able, and active to help me.

Your Word is light to black and gray.

Your Son bears the wounds of my self-inflicted disease and shows the scars of my hateful blows.

Your Son willingly, obediently, faithfully executed Your will to save the likes of me. Why? How? How can you love such a contemptible soul?

How can I be pure in heart?

I do not know. But I ask for pardon, forgiveness, cleansing and beg for Your Spirit to help me in any temptation no matter how insignificant my sin may seem at the time.

~ Your Rest ~
Matthew 11:25–30; 1 Corinthians 1:26–29

Lord of Heaven, Father of all
Ruler, Maker, God, and Sovereign
Why did you reveal Yourself to me?

Not wise, not noble, not strong
No pedigree, no title, no honor
But an orphan, waif, stray, a throwaway

You did not choose
     by man's measure
     by individual accomplishment
     by things contrived on earth

All was handed over to Him
It is well pleasing in Your sight
Only Your Son knows You
Only I know You because You in unequaled kindness
Revealed Yourself to me

Weary of futile work to make righteous
Weary of dos and don'ts
Weary of man-made religions
I welcome Your yoke, Your lessons

It seems I should never ask for more
That I should never impose on You for petty things
Yet you—in great kindness—welcome my requests

So I ask yet for more help
That I find
      Your rest for my soul
      Your easy yoke
      Your light burden

That I remain gentle and humble like You.

~ Before Sin ~

O Sinless One,
    How little awareness we have of that which pulls us
    into sin
    The thoughts that stream through our heads
    The passions that pulse in our hearts
    The distractions that clamor for the attention of
    our desires
    The wounds that somehow justify our choice to rebel.

How easy to see the sins of others
    Their looks
    Their cravings
    Their wicked smiles
    Their free abandon to indulge
    (And the quiet injustice we suffer watching them sin)

Yet we are blind to see—much less admit—
    The temptations of our own looks
    The enticement of our own cravings
    The conception of our own lust that births sin

O Sinless One
    Help me to know the true longings in my soul
    Help me to understand that all sin is an illegitimate
    means to a legitimate end
    Help me to peel back my heart and see that what seems
    to be missing is only and ultimately found in You

And dear God of great comfort
    Help me consider, know, and present myself to You
    Let the joy of intimacy with You outweigh the false
    hope of happiness
    Let the beauty of Your holiness overwhelm the passing
    beauty of this world's offers
    Let the delight of Your friendship fulfill the hollowness
    of friendship with the world

And before I sin,
    Remind me,
    Renew me,
    Knock spiritual sense into me
    So that I do not trade
    The holy for the profane
    The pure for the impure
    The promises for the lies of him who hates me.

"

"WHY ARE YOU SLEEPING?

GET UP AND PRAY

THAT YOU MAY NOT

ENTER INTO TEMPTATION."

—LUKE 22:46

"There's Always One"

My dad has a saying (he has LOTS of sayings) that runs around in my head from time to time. Whenever I complained about people who were "difficult," Dad would respond the same way.

I remember one supervisor at a place I worked. He was in many ways a model employee: He came to work before anyone else in the morning and opened up the business; he worked through lunch and usually stayed later than anyone else. He was very productive—but no one liked him. We tried to stay out of his way, but since he was a supervisor, you ended up dealing with him whether you wanted to or not. I would come home and complain about him to my dad. And Dad would smile and say, "Michael, if he left, they'd replace him. There's always one."

Sure enough, the day came when this guy left. A huge sigh of relief rippled through the place. His successor was a big improvement (as I told my dad, rubbing it in). But in time, other difficult employees came along. So my dad was right again: "There's always one."

I've had a lot of jobs, some better than others, but I've found "there's always one." There's always one who's a hard worker, but stubborn; there's always one who is poor on relational skills; there's always one who speaks her mind and does not care how it makes others feel. There's always one who is, well, a mess.

Proverbs 14:4 notes, "Where no oxen are, the manger is clean, but much revenue comes by the strength of the ox."

If you want a clean stall, you can have it—but you won't get much accomplished. If, however, you want to plow fields, pull wagons, move stones, yank up stumps . . . you need an ox. I don't know for sure, but I would guess that an ox can do the work of, perhaps, ten men. And in many respects, he's a lot easier to care for than ten people. The major problem with the ox is that he makes a lot of muck. He drops it right in the stall, or wherever, and does not care one whit.

So when God, in His delightful sense of humor, drops one of these hardworking but difficult people in your path, focus on the work they accomplish. Focus on their strengths. Focus on whom you'd have to recruit to do their job. Focus on the results they achieve. Focus on the fact that if indeed you got rid of this person, there'd always be "one" to take his place.

As for me, I have a few oxen; and when they drop a load somewhere, it's tempting to get mad. But most of the time I get a shovel instead.

~ Paul on Prayer ~

Tucked inside a section of Paul's letter to the Colossians is a recommendation on prayer. "Devote yourselves to prayer, keeping alert in it with an attitude of thanksgiving" (4:2).

We find here at least three helpful attitudes or dispositions about prayer. First, *Be devoted* which means to continue with something, to persist.

Luke uses the same word in Acts 1:14: "continually devoting themselves to prayer." Paul uses the same term in Romans 12:12: "devoted to prayer." Dr. Luke also records that Jesus was "telling them a parable to show that at all times they ought to pray and not lose heart" (18:1). The idea is a discipline that requires persistence, devotion, and commitment.

Second, *Be alert*. The literal rendering suggests "keeping awake" – vigilance. And as tempting as it is to suggest Paul is referring to a *spiritual* alertness, it seems he is referring to the easy slide into sleep. In Matthew 26:36-41 (and all the synoptic gospels) Jesus tells His disciples to "sit here while I go over there and pray." When He finds them sleeping, He says, "So, you men could not keep watch with Me for one hour?

Third, *Be thankful*. Thankfulness is a choice, a path, a disposition. Isn't it wonderful to be around thankful people?

~ Your Church, Your People ~

O God who called out

You gathered together a people
You called together a people who were not a people
You selected them and loved them
You sustained them from conception

You gave them Your name
You led them with Your Spirit
You protected them with Your hand
You blessed them with Your grace

These, Your people,
    are called by Your name
    are loved by You

Yet these, Your people
    are selfish, stubborn, and sinful
    are critical, resentful, and petty
    are altogether unlovely

Remind me that this is Your church
These are Your people
    You created them
    You called them
    You sent Your Son to die for them

Teach me to be more amazed that I am in Your church
Than to wonder why others are in Your church
Teach me to love Your varied and colorful household
And not to characterize or disdain Your people

Remind me that we are all flesh
Yet You have given Your Spirit
And not to think more highly of myself than I ought to
think
But to love, serve, lead, and encourage
Your church, Your people whom You love and who are
called by Your name.

~ A Preacher's Prayer ~

How can one "preach"?

The task is daunting, the frequency unrelenting.
The preparations are joy, but the crowd of "things" and interruptions nibble away time.
The constant pull of people or preparation, problems or planning
makes second-guessing a way of life.

I long to study.
I long to linger in books and with words.
I love nothing more than being lost in Your Word.
How can the distractions of good and important things be "sanctified" so that study comes later?
How can I say no more often and more graciously to the seemingly needful things?

Give me discipline, that I may be a good steward of time.
Give me focus, that I may concentrate without waver on the matters of the text.
Give me attention, that I may organize so that there is some sense of meaning to Your people.
Above all, give me Your Holy Spirit's control, the only indispensable Agent for communication.

Please help me, Lord, to do all that I can to order my day and time to be a vessel, yet even at that, apart from Your Spirit, it is vain. Help me to do this thing I love, for You, Your people, by Your Spirit, for Your end.

Overcome the limitations of a man and use me in spite of me.

~ A Prayer for My Firstborn ~

Gracious Provider of everything

Please be gracious to my number one
Encourage her heart
Lift her head
Give her eyes to see

You are good when we are not
You are gracious in unseen ways
You are kind when we cannot see
You are loving in all You do

Help this gifted young woman know
That she is deeply loved by You
Deeply loved by her dad
Deeply loved by many who seldom say

Help this young woman, who loves You
To be comforted in disappointments
To be at peace when her world is not
To rest, be still, and know that You are God and You love her

Help her know that
You are forging her into precious metal
You are building an immovable faith
You have used, are using, and will use her in great ways.

Help her rest in her heart of hearts
That in Your eyes she is
Beloved
Beautiful
Gifted
Unique
and has miles yet to travel

Keep her keeping on
Encourage her to press on
Let her know that great things are in Your plans for her.

~ A Leader Asks ~

Our one true Leader

Set apart those who would lead in Your name

May we not
> lead without serving
> neglect your flock
> misuse talents entrusted to us
> lord over those allotted to our charge

May we, by Your gracious sanction
> Serve as You serve
> Care as You care
> Pray as You pray
> Teach as You teach
> Admonish as You admonish
> Be merciful as You are merciful

Help us to submit to You before we lead others
> to know Your wisdom before we decide
> to understand Your Word before we hear opinion
> to acknowledge You and not lean on self
> to hold open and carefully what You have entrusted

Most of all, may our intimacy with You change us
So that all would know:
We have been with Jesus.

Just Plain Stupid

SURELY I AM MORE STUPID THAN ANY MAN,
AND I DO NOT HAVE THE UNDERSTANDING OF A MAN.
NEITHER HAVE I LEARNED WISDOM,
NOR DO I HAVE THE KNOWLEDGE OF THE HOLY ONE.
WHO HAS ASCENDED INTO HEAVEN AND DESCENDED?
WHO HAS GATHERED THE WIND IN HIS FISTS?
WHO HAS WRAPPED THE WATERS IN HIS GARMENT?
WHO HAS ESTABLISHED ALL THE ENDS OF THE EARTH?
WHAT IS HIS NAME OR HIS SON'S NAME?
SURELY YOU KNOW!
PROVERBS 30:2—4

I hate *Jeopardy!* I hate everything about it. My assistant and one of my friends love it. They actually know the questions to most of the answers. I watch it about once a year whether I want to or not. One time, I knew one question. I did see "celebrity *Jeopardy!*" once and thought I might have a chance on that show, with answers such as "red, blue, and yellow are three of these." Or "the largest five-sided office building in the world."

And of course, there's Mr. Smarty-pants-know-it-all Alex Trebek. He actually thinks he knows the questions to all the answers, because he happens to have the questions right in front of him!

When it comes to *Jeopardy!* I am just plain stupid. Which leads me to a guy named Agur.

The only thing we know about Agur, the writer of Proverbs 30, is written in verse 2—a declaration of weariness before God. Why does he call himself "stupid"? In Hebrew it has fields of meaning like "brutish," or "foolish," or perhaps "dull-minded like an animal," in the same sense as it is used in Psalm 73:22: "Then I was senseless and ignorant; I was like a beast before You."

Continuing in verse 2, Agur laments that he does not possess the basic understanding or intellectual ability of "man": Seems like he feels well below average; well below a grade of C minus. He continues this line of thought in verse 3 that he has "neither learned wisdom," nor has he acquired knowledge of the "Holy One." Then in verse 4 he sounds like Job.

In the margin of my Bible at Proverbs 30:2–4 I have written, "I know how you feel, Agur! Me too!!"

I am amazed at some people who seem convinced about everything. One preacher I listen to occasionally is certain about everything. When I listen to him I lament, "I wish I could be as certain about one thing as he is about everything." What gives me joy and hope and energy and a movement from self-deprecating worm theology is the rest of Proverbs 30: For a "stupid" man, Agur pens Scripture. For a dull learner, Agur offers wisdom. And I will get in the dull line over the smart line any day. I've been intimidated by the smart line all my life.

Life is too short to feel stupid. So draw strength from Proverbs 30:5–6: "Every word of God is tested; He is a shield to those who take refuge in Him. Do not add to His words or He will reprove you; and you will be proved a liar."

~ Fools ~

1 Corinthians 1:18–25

Noble Lord, Master of grace,

Hear the prayer of Your foolish worshiper.
Hear, based on the work of the Lord Jesus, the words
measured out from this broken soul.

Listen to the requests from Your adopted child, who asks of
You only because You have granted me permission to ask.
Sift through the ramblings of a poorly prayed request.

Lord, permit me to ask of You. Thank You for listening; for
apart from the Son's perfect work, I could not presume to
have an audience with You.

When the world presses in and mocks my belief and faith in
You, please Lord, embolden me with Your grace, gentleness,
firmness, and holy resolve to smile and communicate
the cross.

When the world hurts and humiliates my belief and faith in
Your word, please Jesus, replace my inability with Your ability.

When the world dismisses me and revels in sin, let me not
hide or cower or rebuke with harsh reaction, but may Your
Spirit control me, my words, my expressions, my countenance and be only and always what You require of me.

When I feel foolish, fearful, and ignorant against the culture's tide of sin, may the only explanation of my response be attributed to You. I am foolish, I am fearful, and I am ignorant, my only hope is in You.

Permit me to be an agent of Your grace, Your gospel, Your cross.

Authorize me to be an ambassador of Your cross, that I may clearly, accurately, with manicured faith, present Christ to the "wise" of this world. May Your Spirit cut through the deceitfulness of all the world offers. May Your Spirit confound the wise, wealthy, powerful, self-made until they see the foolishness of their ways.

You—King of the Universe—know how complete the fool I am. Empower me to communicate, to live, to explain the power and grace of God to deceived, self- worshiping, self-loving, self-serving men and women, who do not even know that they hate You, yet You love them.

~ *Sovereign Father,* ~

Your greatness is unsearchable
Your name is excellent
Your glory is above the heavens.
Ten thousand serve You.
Ten thousand times ten thousand stand before You.

In your awful presence, we are less than nothing.
We do not approach You because we deserve Your notice,
For we are sinners all.

We approach You because
      Our need compels us
      Your Word encourages us
      Our broken hearts remind us
      The Mediator draws us
      Your love motivates us.

Look on us and be merciful to us
Convince us thoroughly of
      Our complete sinfulness
      The penalty of sin due to us
      Our complete pollution of sin within us.

Give us faith to believe, and in believing, life eternal in Jesus
Christ.

May we enter into His sufferings.
Help us to understand Your hand in our grief

Help us to rejoice that they are from Your providence
Let our weeping not hinder our faithfulness
Nor our sorrow obstruct our sanctification.

Be with us to our journey's end
That we may glorify you in life and in death.

We bless You and thank You for
        Preservation, mercy
        Pardon, provision and grace.

We humbly ask You to keep
        evil from us
        health in us
        fear away from us

May we live with a confessing conscience
Cleansed hearts and sound sleep,
Give us a sober and sanctified mind to live for You and
not ourselves.

May we join with Your faithful to recognize
All blessing and honor,
All power and glory,
Belong to the Lamb, Jesus Christ,
The One true Savior and Lord.

Adapted from Valley of Vision, ed. Arthur Bennett, originally entitled
"Third Day Evening: Before Sleep," pp. 388-389 (Carlisle, PA: Banner of
Truth Trust, 1975, 2002). Adapting and editing by Michael J. Easley.

~ A Non-Anxious Presence ~

Resting controlling sovereign Father,

Anxiety in the heart of man weighs down,
But a good word makes it glad.

Patient Master, I need Your rest
    Worry is sin
    Fear is without faith
    Anxiety profits nothing
    Obsession wastes
    Apprehension fritters away

Let me not be deceived in thinking
    My frantic heart is good
    My compulsiveness is useful
    My busyness is spiritual

Please, grant to me a non-anxious presence: in You
I ask You, through Your Spirit to give me a calming presence
    In prayer and study
    In meetings with people You love
    In listening to my family
    In business
    In conversations with friends
    In waiting and being inconvenienced
    In serving You

It will not seem as dramatic as a miracle
It will likely go unnoticed by others
But it will be profound change in a restless heart
It will be soothing oil to an open wound known only to
You and me.

And when I know I am non-anxious
Give me the cognizance to
      Thank You for rest
      Thank You for Your Spirit's help
      Thank You that You heard this anxious prayer.

FIRST OF ALL, THEN, I URGE

THAT ALL ENTREATIES AND

PRAYERS, PETITIONS AND

THANKSGIVINGS, BE MADE

ON BEHALF OF ALL MEN...

—1 TIMOTHY 2:1

Prayer Terms

We approach prayer from many different angles. Some of us come from very religious backgrounds, while others may have had little or no exposure to religious practices. In any case, "religious" practices in and of themselves may not help us understand prayer.

"And when you are praying, do not use meaningless repetition as the Gentiles do, for they suppose that they will be heard for their many words." (Matthew 6:7)

Every time I read Matthew 6:7 it makes me pause. The idea of heaping up lots of names of God or a mantra-like repetition of terms does not make our prayers more acceptable or more religious. The term *meaningless repetition* is one word in the New Testament that essentially means using the same words again and again, to speak without thinking. We have all heard prayers drone on like this and many of us have been guilty of praying this way, too.

In my own prayer life, I have been convicted about the way they all sound the same. I wonder, if you analyzed your prayers, do you say the same thing every time? I imagine if we kept track of our prayer language, we use about fifteen to twenty synonyms every time we pray.

An excellent way to begin studying prayer is to survey Scripture to see the "who, what, where, when, why, and how" of prayer. One helpful exercise for me has been to study the different words used in the Bible that define prayer. I encourage you to do a similar study on your own. Whenever we study words in the Bible, the most important principle is to understand "usage determines meaning." So when a good Bible student says, "this means _____" he or she should be stating that the way the word is used helps us see what it means. So, when you study these terms on your own, look carefully at the context of the passage and ask, "How is the author using the term?"

In the Hebrew Old Testament, we find about twelve words that express prayer. These include. . .

PRAY—*palal* (and related terms) occurs about eighty-four times in the Old Testament. Some of the ways the term is used include praying, confessing, weeping, and prostrating (Ezra 10:1; Isaiah 44:17; 1 Kings 8:33). It might also include the idea of asking God to "judge" as an intercession as in 1 Samuel 2:25. Additionally, the way the term is used includes ideas of "breaking oneself," "being contrite," and "intercession," as with the idea that someone else has to intercede to God on our behalf.

PRAY—*na* is like an entreaty, "I pray," "now," "then," maybe even "Please!" Psalm 118:25 twice we read, "O Lord ... we beseech" (NASB). The ESV retains it, too: "*Save us, we pray, O Lord! O Lord, we pray, give us success!*" (Psalm 118:25, ESV)

PRAYER—*tâphillah* (is related to *palal*) is found about seventy-seven times in the Old Testament. The most frequent usage of this term is found in the Psalms. The first occurrence is in Psalm 4:1. cp. also Psalms 5:3; 6:9; 17:1. Five Psalms use the term in their superscription (Psalms 17, 86,

90, 102, 142.) In 1 Kings 8 and 2 Chronicles 6, the root occurs thirty times.[1]

PETITION—*tâchinnah* also rendered *supplication* in some English versions, seems to have the idea of a request with favor or grace, cp. Jeremiah 37:20; 42:2.

BESEECH—*anna* or *annah* (is related to *na*) found eight times and may suggest an urgency or exigency as in 2 Kings 20:3: "Remember now, O LORD, I beseech You, how I have walked before You in truth and with a whole heart and have done what is good in Your sight." And Hezekiah wept bitterly.[2] Also cp. Nehemiah 1:5. (Nehemiah 1:5-11 is a rich prayer full of significant terms.)

In the New Testament, while we have different Greek words, it is a little harder to draw sharp distinctions in their meaning.

PRAY—*proseuchomai* is found eighty-six times in the New Testament and is technically a petition. The word suggests it came from two words that would literally translate *to wish* or *to pray*. We see the word used in praying for something or for someone. At its simplest form, it is calling on God for some request. (Matthew 6:5-7, 26:42; Acts 1:24, 2:42; Ephesians 6:18; 1 Thessalonians 5:17)

PRAY—*deomai* occurs twenty-two times. In the NASB it is rendered *beseech, implore, beg, begged, pray, please, request*. While *proseuchomai* and *deomai* could be seen as synonyms and in some ways could be used interchangeable, *deomai* may suggest that the one praying lacks something, is in need of something, is in want. We can be sure that it has the sense of asking or seeking. (Matthew 9:38; Luke 5:12, 8:28; Hebrews 5:7; 1 Thessalonians 3:10)

ASK—*aiteo* occurs forty-eight times. It does not always mean asking in the sense of praying. Most intriguing, when Jesus used the term, it was only in referencing others' prayers, not His own (John 16:26). It may be that this term reflects the petitioner's request for him/herself.

PRAY—*euchomai* is found seven times in the New Testament. Four of the occurrences are specific to prayer (2 Corinthians 13:7, 9; 3 James 5:16; John 2). Along with the meaning of prayer, we also find the word used as a *wish*. Not a wish upon some object, but a desirable outcome that we would pray for, such as a wish a person would come to faith in Christ (Romans 9:3; Acts 26:29).

Prayer Attitudes

In addition to different terms, we also need to see the different categories, or, perhaps better, attitudes of prayer. Many of these are easy to identify in the Psalms.

LAMENT—the petitioner expresses mourning or grief. It may be personal or national (Psalms 3, 4, 13, 77; 1 Samuel 1:17ff). The language includes complaint, lament, petition, and essentially a crying out to God for help in dealing with enemies, sickness, drought, and the results of sin and guilt.

PRAISE—an expression of value and worth (Psalms 8, 19, 33, 145-150). By the very nature of the word, we are ascribing praise, value, and worth to the One alone who is deserving. We praise God for His character, kindness, mercy, grace (all His attributes are praiseworthy), and ultimately for His Son. He alone provides our deliverance. He provides rescue. He grants forgiveness. He hears our prayers and this should evoke praise in the heart and response of the worshiper.

WORSHIP—though similar to praise, we might differentiate worship as a more comprehensive response from the believer to God. Our very lives are to be worship to God (Romans 12:1-2). Our approach, our praise, the focal point of worship is that we adore the Holy Sovereign Lord. Perhaps the most elegant expression of this is seen in Revelation 4-5. As hard as it is to simplify the concept of worship in our prayers, we are getting close when our focus, life, service, and affections are on Him and not ourselves. He is the only One worthy of worship.

THANKSGIVING—is a crucial component in our worship and prayer (Jeremiah 33:11; Ephesians 5:20; Colossians 3:17; Hebrews 13:15). Focusing on who God is and what He has done are ways to remind us of our need to be thankful. Note Philippians 4:6-7, "... with thanksgiving ..."

CONFESSION—our need for forgiveness is integral to prayer. Even for those who have trusted Christ and Christ alone for their salvation need the ongoing forgiveness from sin. To confess is to admit or concede, as in 1 John 1:9. But there are other important aspects to confession, including admit (Matthew 3:6), *profess allegiance* (Philippians 2:11), *give thanks* (Luke 10:21), and *praise* (Romans 15:9).

Prayer Postures

Seldom do we vary the posture of our prayers. I do not think there is a "right" or "wrong" way to pray, but we do see several different physical prayer postures in Scripture. Examples abound, I have only given a small sample for each.

KNEELING

Now Solomon had made a bronze platform...and had set it in the midst of the court; and he stood on it, knelt on his knees in the presence of all the assembly of Israel and spread out his hands toward heaven. (2 Chronicles 6:13)

For this reason I bow my knees before the Father. (Ephesians 3:14)

PROSTRATE

Abram fell on his face, and God talked with him, saying ... (Genesis 17:3)

"I fell down before the Lord, as at the first, forty days and nights; I neither ate bread nor drank water, because of all your sin which you had committed in doing what was evil in the sight of the Lord to provoke Him to anger." (Deuteronomy 9:18)

And He went a little beyond them, and fell on His face and prayed, saying, "My Father, if it is possible, let this cup pass from Me; yet not as I will, but as You will." (Matthew 26:39)

And the twenty-four elders, who sit on their thrones before God, fell on their faces and worshiped God. (Revelation 11:16)

Now while Ezra was praying and making confession, weeping and prostrating himself before the house of God, a very large assem-

bly, men, women, and children, gathered to him from Israel; for the people wept bitterly. (Ezra 10:1)

BOWED

"And I bowed low and worshiped the Lord, and blessed the Lord, the God of my master Abraham, who had guided me in the right way to take the daughter of my master's kinsman for his son." (Genesis 24:48)

So the people believed; and when they heard that the Lord was concerned about the sons of Israel and that He had seen their affliction, then they bowed low and worshiped. (Exodus 4:31)

Now at the completion of the burnt offerings, the king and all who were present with him bowed down and worshiped. Moreover, King Hezekiah and the officials ordered the Levites to sing praises to the Lord with the words of David and Asaph the seer. So they sang praises with joy, and bowed down and worshiped. (2 Chronicles 29:29–30)

STANDING

She said, "Oh, my lord! As your soul lives, my lord, I am the woman who stood here beside you, praying to the Lord." (1 Samuel 1:26)

"Whenever you stand praying, forgive, if you have anything against anyone, so that your Father who is in heaven will also forgive you your transgressions." (Mark 11:25)

"The Pharisee stood and was praying this to himself: 'God, I thank You that I am not like other people: swindlers, unjust, adulterers, or even like this tax collector. 'I fast twice a week; I pay tithes of all that I get.' But the tax collector, standing some distance away, was even unwilling to lift up his eyes to heaven, but was beating his

breast, saying, 'God, be merciful to me, the sinner!' " (Luke 18:11–13)

LIFTING HANDS

Then Ezra blessed the Lord the great God. And all the people answered, 'Amen, Amen!" while lifting up their hands; then they bowed low and worshiped the Lord with their faces to the ground. (Nehemiah 8:6)

Hear the voice of my supplications when I cry to You for help, when I lift up my hands toward Your holy sanctuary. (Psalm 28:2)

Therefore I want the men in every place to pray, lifting up holy hands, without wrath and dissension. (1 Timothy 2:8)

[1]Cp. Harris, R. L., Harris, R. L., Archer, G. L., & Waltke, B. K. (1999, c1980). *Theological Wordbook of the Old Testament* (electronic ed.) (Page 726). Chicago: Moody Press.

MASTERING THE ART OF

PRAYER, LIKE ANYTHING ELSE,

TAKES TIME. THE TIME

WE GIVE IT WILL BE A TRUE

MEASURE OF ITS IMPORTANCE

TO US.

—J. OSWALD SANDERS

~ Passion & Anger ~

Holy Lord,

How little repentance there is in the world, and how many sins I have to repent of!

I am troubled for my sin of passion, for the shame and horror of it as an evil;

I purpose to give way to it no more, and come to You for strength to that end.

Most men give vent to anger frequently and are overcome by it, bringing many excuses and attenuation for it,
so that it occurs suddenly,
that they delight not in it,
that they are sorry afterwards,
that godly men commit it.
They seek peace after outbursts of passion by entire forgetfulness of it, or, by skimming over their wound, they hope for healing without peace in Christ's blood.

Lord God, I know that my sudden anger arises when things cross me, and I desire to please only myself, not Christ;
There is in all wrongs and crosses a double cross—that which crosses me, and that which crosses You;
In all good things there is something that pleases me, something that pleases You.

So, I am like Eli, the subject of punishment for not rebuking sin,
when I should humbly confess my sin and fly to the blood of Christ for pardon and peace.

Give me, then, repentance, true brokenness, lasting contrition, for these things You will not despise in spite of my sin.

~ O Great Physician ~

Healer, Comforter, Father of mercy
We often ask You to ease our pain
> To cure our illnesses
> To heal our diseases
> To free us from suffering
Yet we remain sick

Please help us, we pray
> To know if our sin has made us sick
> When we must live as invalids, with no relief in sight,
> To know that we may have to suffer, endure,
> and be joyful

Forgive us,
> When our sickness is what makes our pleading
> urgent—
> Rather than simply our longing to be with You
> When we repent only because we search for cures
> When we are angry, depressed, or injure others
> because we suffer
> When we wound those who try to help

Refocus our fixation
> Help us pray for our physicians, nurses, family,
> and friends
> Who must convalesce with us
> Help us, through new eyes of compassion, to see
> others who suffer

Help us suffer well because we are truly healed
Help us share our eternal hope in Christ with those
who suffer without Him

Let us not be
... Hezekiah and pray for long life
... Asa and only turn to physicians
... Job's wife and speak with contempt
... Jonah and long to die

Let us be like Paul, who chose contentment
And most like Jesus, who suffered obediently.

Thank You
... when the fever leaves
... when the pain subsides
... when we sleep well

Remind us always that we are a diseased people
That all pain is due the Fall
That all grief-sting is temporary, though it feels forever
And that You, the great Physician, heal our most
terminal disease.

Make us know we do not have to get better to be well.

EVERY TIME WE PRAY,

OUR HORIZON IS ALTERED,

OUR ATTITUDE TO THINGS

IS ALTERED, NOT SOMETIMES

BUT EVERYTIME, AND THE

AMAZING THING IS THAT

WE DON'T PRAY MORE.

—OSWALD CHAMBERS

Eye on the Ball

LET YOUR EYES LOOK DIRECTLY AHEAD
AND LET YOUR GAZE BE FIXED STRAIGHT IN FRONT OF YOU.
WATCH THE PATH OF YOUR FEET.
AND ALL YOUR WAYS WILL BE ESTABLISHED.
PROVERBS 4:25—26

It's amazing how easily our heads are turned. I can walk across a parking lot, and many harmless things turn my head. I can drive home, and many not-so-harmless things turn my head. I can plan and dream and pray, and many things can pull my attention from my task. I think I have a major case of spiritual ADD and ADHD.

I love the words of these verses. "Directly ahead." Not turned, letting my eyes graze on other fields. "Fixed straight in front of you." Deliberate, focused, intent. Eye on the ball. There's a lot to be said for a single, clear focus.

Hang tough. Stay true. Live and think clean.

~ Remind Me ~

O great God of grace
Remind me of the time of my salvation
Renew my memory to my desperate condition
Recall in my soul the terminal illness that I inherited
From my great ancestor, Adam.

Remind me of the cost of my salvation
Renew my forgetful memory to Gethsemane, the cross,
the cries of separation
Recall in my soul that He loved You, obeyed You, and
healed the incurable illness
And was and is the great Second Adam.

Remind me that I am not here for myself
Repair my penchant for seeing life "all about me"
Refocus my vision away from me toward You
The greatest lover of my soul

Remind me to live for You
Reawaken childlike faith that wants to please You
Rekindle a simple devotion that crowds out self
And longs to be with You, to know You, to rest in You

Remind me every day, I am not my own
Regenerate my spiritual life to that which is spiritual
Restore to me the joy of my salvation
That I will joyfully serve You, Your kingdom
And Your righteousness

~ *Like a Dead Man* ~

You are
    The Son of Man
    The One clothed in white, girded with gold
    The One whose head and hair are white
    The One with eyes of fire and feet of burnished bronze
    The One with a voice like many strong waters
    The First and the Last
    The Living One who was dead
    The One with the keys of death and Hades[3]

And when we see you, we will fall on our faces like dead men.

What is man, that You take thought of him
And the son of man, that You care for him?[4]

I am
    Consumed with me (all the time)
    Preoccupied with my (anything)
    Fearful of what might affect me
    Anxious about health
    Gathering money
    Busy with important things
    Restless with "what-ifs"

What is man, that You take thought of him
And the son of man, that You care for him?

When will I be what You want?
When will I
Serve like You served
Love like You loved
See others like You see
Know that I am Yours and not mine?

Please help . . .
Because every time I get any glimpse of You
All I do is fall on my face like a dead man.

[3] *Revelation 1:13–18*
[4] *Psalm 8:4*

I HAVE OFTEN LEARNED

MORE IN ONE PRAYER

THAN I HAVE BEEN

ABLE TO GLEAN

FROM MUCH READING

AFTER REFLECTION.

— MARTIN LUTHER

What Happens When You Talk?

A WORD FITLY SPOKEN
IS LIKE APPLES OF GOLD IN A SETTING OF SILVER.
LIKE A GOLD RING OR AN ORNAMENT OF GOLD
IS A WISE REPROVER TO A LISTENING EAR.
PROVERBS 25:11—12, ESV

A physician friend of mine epitomizes this Proverb. He was skilled in all manner of speech. I used to watch him in elder meetings, and he would ask the right questions and cut to the chase, but he did it in remarkable fashion. Kind words. Wise words. Hard questions, softly asked.

I am not very good in the heat of the battle. I get emotional, say things emotionally; I would be a lousy poker player. Yet wisdom is deep, and it knows how to keep cool. It knows how to say the right words in the right setting. It knows how to say hard things softly. It knows how to look a person in the eye with love, firmness, confidence, and compassion—apples of gold in settings of silver—all at once. I marvel when I come across these kinds of folks. I want to be like that.

Verse 12 promises the rewards of being a person who has the right way of saying things. When you are able to speak this way, when you have to "reprove" someone, the person will listen. The implication is not only will he or she listen, they will learn. Wouldn't it be great if we were so wise, kind, elegant in wisdom and words that when we spoke, people actually listened and learned?

God, give me that kind of wisdom, Holy Spirit's control, to embroider words that honor You.

~ Hating Sin, Loving Him ~

How can I love the world that hated Him?
How can I love the sin that drove Him to Calvary?
How can I look twice at that which required His Holy Life?

Gracious Master and my God, help me to
    Worship You acceptably
    Serve You eagerly
    Long for You frequently
And to know that You are better than anything this world
may offer.

May I see that any longing for power, prosperity, or pleas-
antry is contrary to longing for You.
May I see that nothing this world can ever offer, tempt or
tantalize is better than You and You alone.

May I see that my sins have far greater impact than I want
to acknowledge.
And may I see that Your forgiveness has far greater impact
than I can understand.

Dear gracious Master and my Savior, help me to
    Pray joyfully
    Rest contentedly
    Live faithfully
And to know and experience that hating sin is loving You.

~ Strong God ~

Eternal and strong God
Merciful and lovingkind
We praise You for Your great strength and mercy
Toward those who
> love You
> fear You
> worship You
> long to serve You
> but far, far too often sin against You.

You have been and continue to be our stronghold
You allowed us safe passage through long nights of our
lost voyage
And greeted us with the morning of our salvation.

You protected us from destruction when we traveled
treacherous waters
> too close to reefs of death
> too deep in storms of sin
And you patiently nudged us toward Your strong winds
and safe harbors.

We would never have seen the danger of our self-
destructive course
We would never have known the tragedies You prevented
Unless You in Your eternal strength had stayed the
onslaught of sin and death.

In the strength You have given me (for I have no other)
help me to
      talk of You
      praise You
      make known Your strength,
      The One who saved me from certain and
      eternal judgment.

~ Creator's Art ~
Psalm 8:1–9

One Creator
Perfect Designer
Forgive me for missing Your art

Only the road do my eyes see
Only the labor does my mind think
"All about me" blocks the view

Compel me to consider Your handiwork
Lift my eyes at night to see Your stellar wonder
All suspended in their courses

Awaken my dulled senses to Your palette
Open my eyes to the seasons of Your delight
Unique with color, beauty, terror, life, and death

Provoke my recall of Your designs
Prod my thoughts of marvelous memories
Ocean's edges, mountain's crags, river's rage

And when my perspective must be level
Draw my lines to that which matters
Sharpen my vision of Your image bearers

~ Earth's Threshold ~

Broken, failing, tiring,
Shrinking, aging, fading

The journey takes its toll
        The battle its casualties
        The disease its victims
And Your hands turn our faces toward night.

The end unsettles
        The young deny it
        We repress it
        The aged fear it

When did growing become dying?
        Vitality become weary?
        Potential become nostalgia?
        Ideas become indifferent?

The unwelcome guest too soon comes
        Without invitation
        Lacking respect
        Seldom without notice
        He knocks on the door

Creatures for eternity, yet fallen flesh
Clinging to the *now*, pensive of *then*
We all must depart

Add all moments of the past
To equal only this moment
The earthbound threshold is ever there
    Only one step
    Only one direction
    Only one time

Yet You, the Great One, await
    Across the way
    On the other shore
    In the new realm

Conqueror of death, disease, pain, and sin
Justifier, Redeemer, Priest, and Friend
Father, Savior, Protector, and Judge
Help me live well, and step across the final threshold
Full of life and faith.

Acknowledgments

A generous thanks to *Moody Publishers* for their kind encouragement to go to print with this project. Thanks especially to Greg Thornton, Betsey Newenhuyse, and Dave DeWit for their considerable contributions in editing, design, and style. *Soli deo gloria*.

About the Author

Michael J. Easley began serving as president of Moody Bible Institute on March 1, 2005. He is a graduate of Stephen F. Austin State University, where he received a bachelor of science in education in 1980, and Dallas Theological Seminary, where he received a master of theology in 1985 and a doctor of ministry in 2003. In recognition of his doctoral work, the seminary awarded Dr. Easley the John G. Mitchell Award for outstanding scholarship and effectiveness in ministry.

Prior to assuming the presidency of MBI, Dr. Easley served in pastoral ministry for twenty years. He began as a youth pastor intern at Trinity Fellowship in Dallas, Texas, before becoming senior pastor of Grand Prairie Bible Church in Grand Prairie, Texas. After nine years at Grand Prairie Bible, he was appointed senior pastor of Immanuel Bible Church in Springfield, Virginia, outside Washington, D.C., where he served for more than eleven years. Since 1993, Dr. Easley and his wife, Cindy, have also spoken together at FamilyLife marriage conferences. Dr. Easley and Cindy met in college and married in 1980. They have four children: Hanna, Jessie, Devin, and Sarah.

SINCE 1894, Moody Publishers has been dedicated to equip and motivate people to advance the cause of Christ by publishing evangelical Christian literature and other media for all ages, around the world. Because we are a ministry of the Moody Bible Institute of Chicago, a portion of the proceeds from the sale of this book go to train the next generation of Christian leaders.

If we may serve you in any way in your spiritual journey toward understanding Christ and the Christian life, please contact us at www.moodypublishers.com.

"All Scripture is God-breathed and is useful for teaching, rebuking, correcting and training in righteousness, so that the man of God may be thoroughly equipped for every good work."
—2 TIMOTHY 3:16, 17

MOODY
PUBLISHERS
THE NAME YOU CAN TRUST®